The Draw of Broken Eyes
& Whirling Metaphysics

Alan,

You are an angel
in this mad world.

Your friend,

THE DRAW OF BROKEN EYES
& WHIRLING METAPHYSICS

POEMS

CLIFFORD BROOKS

SECOND EDITION

SCE Press

Jasper, Georgia

SCE Press
Jasper, Georgia

Revisions have been made to some of the poems since the first edition of
the book published by John Gosslee Books, 2012.

The poems "The Sudden, Angry Sky" and "I Saw the Klan Today" were
reprinted in *Calamaro Magazine* after publication of the book's first
edition.

ISBN: 978-1-7347498-3-0 - Paperback
eISBN: 978-1-7347498-4-7 - ePub
eISBN: 978-1-7347498-5-4 - Mobi

Printed in the United States of America   10 9 8 7 6 5 4 3 2
0 9 1 4 2 0

⊗This paper meets the requirements of ANSI/NISO Z39.48-1992
(Permanence of Paper)

Author photo by James Polfuss
Front cover design by Laura McCullough
Font: Georgia

for Momma, Daddy, Chris Davis,
Greg Hosmer, Travis Key, and Hailey Fleming.

CONTENTS

II. Whirling Metaphysics

III. The Gateman's Hymn of Ignoracium

Foreword to the Second Edition

This extraordinary book of poetry was greeted with a Pulitzer Prize nomination after the first edition was released by John Gosslee Books in 2012. It was written by one of the South's native sons (he grew up in Crawford, Georgia) whose passion for writing is exceeded only by his passion for life. He has lived hard and loved strong, and has a gift of language that will touch your soul.

I first met Clifford Brooks in Jasper, Georgia in 2013, shortly after *The Draw of Broken Eyes & Whirling Metaphysics* was published. We sat down one day over sushi to discuss the world of letters. I was doing a profile of him for the local paper and he was planning a book tour for the release. We met for lunch that day, and it was clear he'd had a long night of it.

It was not until later that I found out that most of Clifford's nights are long. This suffering insomniac, who openly speaks of his medication, his past struggles with addiction, and his passion-filled, life-on-the-edge existence, is showing no signs of slowing as he enters his forties. He writes in "The Soma of a Fevered Condition": "Night needs no introduction as I adore everything after midnight."

It is this passion—unpredictable, rich, contagious—that will draw you into the tender poems of the first section, "The Draw of Broken Eyes," poems that not only reflect his childhood and young-adult years but also the lessons they taught him. You will experience the loss of love ("You are the catalyst / and the razor, / the haunting *I can't remember*."), the pain of regret ("a road has stolen her closeness to me. / the door is flung open /

with nothing outside but / a humid afternoon."), and the longing for redemption ("reminding a sinner / home is home, / even alone.")

The remainder of the book includes what Clifford says is sort of a re-creation of his days working with the Department of Juvenile Justice in rural northwest Georgia. These poems will sting you with their honesty and shock you with their insight. "There's a 3 AM bleakness / to some people," he writes in "Midnight Alley Wolves," which you can't help but think is part autobiographical, part observer. The final section, "The Gateman's Hymn of Ignoracium," will shake your insides. After a haunting tirade on the brutalities he found in juvenile social work, Brooks concludes with a vicious and resounding victory for society's most vulnerable victims.

One of the things that separates Clifford from his fellow poets is the endless energy he invests in others. About 10 years ago he began thinking about a way to bring artists together—not an easy task, given that many artists take serious pride in their independence and wear their non-conformity like a badge of honor. It wasn't long before he started the Southern Collective Experience, a group of hand-chosen creative artists including musicians, playwrights, poets, and visual artists who meet informally to share their talents. From that group has come the *The Blue Mountain Review* and the NPR radio show *Dante's Old South,* and many other professional opportunities for these artists .

Clifford's energy often drives him to the literary edge, but it also serves to inspire an entire community of artists. He said recently on his radio show that he wants to "challenge the boundaries" of traditional thought, particularly on how we look at poetry and the possibilities it provides. He has called the Collective "my greatest joy."

Clifford's family roots are strong. He is the third Charles Clifford Brooks, and he maintains close ties to his ancestral home in Lexington, Georgia, where he hosts events for his Southern Collective Experience colleagues and other artists.

He is a frequent guest at poetry workshops, and many a night you can find him reading his work to an audience spellbound by both his presence and his verse.

When I first met Clifford during that lunch five years ago, he signed a copy of this remarkable book with "This is our future, so buckle up and get ready." We are ready, as Brooks' future will always be one step ahead of the literary curve.

David R. Altman, 2018

David R. Altman, an Ohio native who resides in Lawrenceville, Georgia, was nominated for Georgia Author of the Year in Poetry for his 2014 chapbook *Death in the Foyer* (Finishing Line Press). He has had poems published in *The American Journal of Poetry* and *The Blue Mountain Review*. Altman is the Books & Writers Editor of a small north Georgia weekly paper, the *Pickens County Progress* in Jasper, Georgia.

And when Love speaks, the voices of all the gods make heaven drowsy with its harmony.

—WILLIAM SHAKESPEARE

There is one thing one has to have: either a soul that is cheerful by nature, or a soul made cheerful by work, love, art, and knowledge.

—FRIEDRICH NIETZSCHE

Some friendships do not last, but some friends are more loyal than brothers.

Proverbs 18:24

I. The Draw of Broken Eyes

Ode to Morning Glories

Morning glories crept up
to the balcony,
stowaways in a canna lily.

You blossom as soon
as your sister wilts.

Among the African violets
and swollen jade,
  you are queens.

A Mountain Town

After violins reminded the elderly
of my abundant youth,
I went out into a drizzle.
I've got dreams, came between drags,
dreams to remember....

The light from windows held me,
hiding the evening sky.
Feeling the chill of a cerebellum slipping,
these old homes seemed sturdy.

A mountain town was serene
as my wandering walk home
got lost in a dark wood.

Shouldering Divorce

I handled it all wrong:

The days locked away,
thinking of Yeats
instead of you.

Scowling hours not eating,
too dour to dive in
and struggle us
out of drowning.

Too much Huck
to hang around,
I did nothing.
The whole thing
went off wrong.

Cerebral Reverb

Shoulders twist at odd angles
as synapse-to-synapse snap.
The throat barks
where it didn't before.
My muscles so mangled
toes curl.

One professor
in Abnormal Psychology,
a cat with the most
brilliant comb over,
called them *tics*.

Now Strauss spreads out
over vinyl
to bring me down,
but my calm is a calamity.
Hair covers my
knotting neck.

I don't shave
so my mouth
isn't seen creaking.
I am a marionette
stricken with tangled strings.

A Raven in Memoriam

Winged, earth-whipped, eyes too wide,
a storm of cackles careens
from barren trees.
Chest a muscle poured out,
he is eaten with the rasping chant,
I promise. I promise. I promise.

Go onward into the city,
over the distracted crowd,
jump! (up, Up, UP)
Raven feathers glint and flitter
like spastic,
unwatched children.

. . .

Plumage juts out of my elbows,
spreads across the ribcage
from my spine.
This body's brutal allure
is not healthy.
It's to hide, attempting to ignore
you, a tryst.

Leave.
The last Lady Chatterley's room
was just churned up
and hocked out,
ready to make a place
beneath my glossy breast
for anything but
another girl's hungry presence.

I don't deny
the gashed-open heart is laughable,
that the wicked end is sweeter.
Over lips she slips
to the edge of my ear.
She tells me I sparkle, that I'm full of mercury.
What are you thinking?
How do you feel about me?

I feel you should get out of my bed.
I fear that my sticky-pitch feathers
will cling to you,
litter the ground,
lead you back to my
clutch of earth
where another isn't needed.
Your teeth taste some dangerous life
I swear isn't here.

August in a Bad Place

I haven't fumbled over you in weeks,
these previous roundings of night's
great, white eye.
The taste of cherries, rum,
the pick-to-the-sternum epiphany
you've probably misplaced me.
The root of my unease is in hours
debating with lizards, admiring fruit,
puzzling over why moths and butterflies
cover saints.

A mirage was born, us.
Incubated, chiseled,
an exercise in having something else
on my mind.

How did she spend Mardi Gras?
What did she do before me?
Maybe love isn't enough like God.

Flipping through pictures
of you in uniform, in sunglasses, blowing kisses,
I keep them close.
Gone, gone, gone – I hear the world differently,
shuffling like a vagrant,
Thorazine-stoned.

I couldn't think you were still in
thistled veins *whooshed* out.
You wanted me to come,
not knowing how, where you were,
how much time you had.

Better Africa than here, I decided.
You had to go. Save
what's nowhere near.

[Groaning alone,
sitting in the shower,
pounded by hot water.]

Conversations with Daisy

Daisy saunters through tulips, lights,
wearing an expression worn thin
by eight years
of conflicted evenings.

> Cherokee rose blooms around his crown.
> A photo fills her absence from the dashboard.
> *Go faster! Go farther!*
> Leave the throng for the baby girl
> looking for a man who knows her tendons,
> doubts and daydreams.
> The lies where you are get worse.

Roaring, sex of the starving,
sucked up on waking this morning,
has long worn off.
The memory of tongues
and breath against the glass of a '69 Chevelle,
she never bothers with underthings.
Tonight, this cowboy,
listening to "Lacrimosa,"
coasts through Georgia.

> *A Millay without the burden*
> *of old rain,*
> *practicing the Merengue to keep control,*
> *she pulls on her skirt*
> *both gent- and thug-owned.*
> *Take note the cut of her hip, her libido*
> *slicing a stranger's judgment, anticipating the last call.*

Donne, Williams and Stevens:
There have been miles upon miles
from the crossroads
to Devil's Pond,

now in-between.
Making a rhythm
with thumbs on the steering wheel,
her spread-out scent
is in his nucleus.

The Sudden, Angry Sky

Storms are a howling wave.
Now rain heaves
over the roof.
Dogs huddle beneath houses.
Lightning rears up horses.
The tempest has a grudge.

Prayer

All of us
are born from sparrows;
a string of dreams.
Grow firmly between
rocks and roots,
dear muses.
Sway as
wind brings spring.

Supernal watchmen
wish we would notice
their urge to join
"By and by, Lord,
By and by."

Let's woo 'em into our fold
and sing "Redemption Song."
We rowdy few
shall rejoice,
and throw dice
with angels.

Hallowed Ground

An old house
shrouded by magnolia trees
has an endless stairway
which looks back
at its turning point
on this stranger
smelling of grandfather's clothes.

Late Saturday

With faces full of
unkempt hunting, craving
for love, for sex, for sleep,
we are divided
by an asylum
in Washington State.

From the front door,
neighbors keep pounding and pounding
and pounding.
Letting in those guests
is not release,
never a girl.

It's been 39 days.

I struggle,
feel bound,
squeezed shut in the lungs
of some petty beast.

. . .

The air is hemmed with hyacinth.
In thick blue and pink petals,
perfume triggers
the whisper:

I don't know where she is.

Melody Between the Moon and Earth

part one

Our heritage is the meadow,
the bursting apple
point of rupture where
there are no more
cases of breakage.

Only the sound of insects,
finches fussing at one another,
my bare shoulders and your smooth calves
worshiping the sun.

part two

I am no bereaved elder-creator looking
to God,
then the sand,
for a secret of first breath.

You.
It is you.

Now, from the space around stars
there's a hope
that the sacrifice
of you being so far away
will become a healed wound.

part three

You are the warm tongue
on my jaw, the tickle,
the melody
between the moon and earth.

finding miss mary

little miss mary,
i hold a bit of you
beneath glass,
a marble misplaced
beneath your baby grand,

an iridescent cat's eye,
and hear you whisper,
you're precious, sugar.
a music box plays mozart.

Wolves

This addiction
and
that pale glow

resolute,
swaggering,
bristling.

They are
echoes
of honest men.

6:00 AM

Running a hand over feral hair,
waking is a drop-kick to the balls.
December dons
a grey suit.
The ceiling sags.

The room's view:
an empty playground,
pigeons,
beer bottles,
brittle grass.

Smelling of tea roses
and worry,
time is perpetually blurry.
Christmas is nothing
but ghosts.

Taking Up the Road

Taking up the road
to a home that wasn't
so kind before,
I only have more to regret,
and a worse habit.

First: childhood.
The soundtrack
ran from the Motown dad spun
to grunge.
Secondly I got tossed
out for my family's comfort.

On the third return
I came to swoon over she
who adored me
best boozed up.

Now there are Jamaicans
with lonely days closing,
and Athens
is my catastrophic
New Orleans.

saturday afternoon at hilton head

sit up, ladybug! salt-licked skin preserves sneaky
kisses
to endure over lighthouses, state lines,
reveling last night to sprawl out this morning.

linen long sleeve shirts still show body art,
damaged wrists, muscles
strained, pushing veins close to flesh;
the last five years
have been barren.

sea life leaps upward, her thighs,
his fingertips
dolphins between breasts shaped like teardrops
pink from sighs and stretching.
neptune's trident
fuses
the two's pressed sexes.

water swells bedclothes into the corner
where a guitar and thigh-high boots lean
from yesterday afternoon.
pages are strewn like sand dollars, ink dried,
splashed with pineapple juice and lipstick.

seagulls squawk at children
while a ceiling fan whips hot air
around the bedroom.
hard world is at a terrific distance,
farther, farther, farther
until an island stretch
is wed to the sky.

it's a flavor of madness,
of strawberries,
of what is.

overnight

above the roof is an expanse
fitting winter.
there is no noise,
only distance
between
flesh
and
fresh nettles.

little of the sapphire
thread of earth-splitting
long swamp creek
found north
is here.
tonight there's only snow
reflecting back
a starless space.

no animals make
quick tracks,
sleeping now in burrows.
silence between clustered
pines is pierced
by an ambulance.
le coeur bat bat
bat bat
bat bat.

The Soma of a Fevered Condition

Initial hellos were straight-to-bedroom innuendo, strained, already blessed with an expiration date, disdain, differences, fucking for the only good reason. I almost-loved, I kind-of-loved, I half-loved debutantes who held an auburn curl to escape while I mumbled bad sonnets. Both of us bathed in a backwards notion nuptials lingered near. I am unfair, unjust: these attempts at passion were hopeful photons that collided in their/our minds and cast us as eternal, though we were not. Romantics are blind clowns faced away from the audience. The big grin and frantic hands, the make-up and bow tie are unseen by those seated; unnoticed, unimportant to the gaudy performer—all laughter sounds the same.

Night needs no introduction as I adore everything after midnight. The best maiden, breasts and faith exposed, is genuine. The closest star manufactures a slamming effect that bangs my nerves out of steel and into sandpaper. I find few helpful jinn when skies are blurred by senses always too receptive to focus. Provide me a small, white cup with wafers water washes down to make all this palatable, carpet more comfortable, the conditional affection of one lady with a ravenous need to test me less repugnant.

Jealous room searches are finally curbed today as we're apart for all time, every day, sharing space while wanting more of it. I no longer lie to buy music; to stay with friends equally deep in cartoons. Forget grabbing volcano rolls after a movie and home by 9 PM. We were/are car crashes of stubborn will, unable to heal. No sugar to settle a stomach too hot to hold food, calories gone, a stalemate rages between anorexia and mom's uneasy life of worry. What is the melody made to remind this tyrant he can't cheat Charon, that he is vulnerable, that he should sell the pistol in his nightstand? No soundtrack for some slackers—*What's my responsibility?*

Conditioned towards paranoia, self-conscious, owing I'm sorry
too often, foolish over weakness, this wicked last year, my
penchant to use, and use, and use. *Morphine is a fan of
forgetfulness.* Reading about compulsive disorders, night terrors,
and grinding teeth there is the truth it may not get better, always
lack sex, never become an oasis. Away from here, eager for
nothing, I'm determined to see only daisies, hear only Vivaldi,
ignore any more tedious stories.

Kneeling by the River

In this stream
the current is freezing.
God looks through this conduit
without ill will or culpability,
just smiles
and gets to business.

brevity

strip the geranium
to one petal.
shave words to their marrow.
the meaning lasts.
simplicity is our crux.

Lavender

part one

Now:

The sky is furious.
Air conditioners echo across the courtyard.
A shirtless old man
smokes black cigarettes.

I haven't planted anything.
My jade can't
find the right light.

Days tear out
free of incident.
It's practice.
It lacks a feline curve.

Lavender wafts from somewhere.
Maybe the Hindus
upstairs burn incense.
Flowers open
thinking.

The fact I imagine a companion
does nothing
to fill my desolate bed.
Prayers seem to throw
words into a void.
At least that's how it looks
from here.

part two

Later:

A heat storm has fingers
the length of Cadillac parades
that wrap beneath clouds' bellies.
Humidity is the co-host
to the question, will you ever depart?
Her lavender lotion
is on my clothes.

Restlessness,
yes.
Legs and arms tan, laying out
on lawn chairs,
bickering over
peach cobbler ice cream

Pilgrimage

In Lúnasa I went for a stroll
to buy peanuts and a Coke.
Alone except for dust and loose stones,
pines cut a cool line ahead.
Their shade was a friend
against summer's hard stare.

I rambled, rambled, rambled on.
Looking beyond lazy cattle,
a pond dotted by cattails
and dragonflies.
Turtles soothed on warm rocks.

To my left spread out a buddleia.
Two Monarchs sifted through
its ivory-bundled blossoms.
I spied the randomness in their routine.

I neglected to notice until then
the scarcity of these ballerinas.
Spring azures,
swallowtails, and lacework whites
were late.
Maybe a deluge
washed away too many cocoons.
Perhaps they overslept.

Ahead, an old trading post—
commerce off a rarely-traveled road.
The exterior, like its attendant,
was weathered.
A cigar store Indian stood guard
over this magnanimous, God-fearing man.

"Hot enough for ya'?" he asked
from under a hat's faded logo.
"It's not so bad." I nodded in return.

Back outside with a Coke
and the salt of peanuts,
I hid in shadows,
scuttled away from the flames.

Rain

Sunflowers snake upward
around the brittle remains
of an azalea. Birds break shells
& throw life.

. . .

Here:
Lounge chairs for star gazing,
ashtrays,
match sticks
in a box for coffin nails.
No wind chimes.
Not a single piece of folk art.

Before the young men
of Dixie go in - pause - lungs & smoke.
Pregnant clouds ease towards
late afternoon.
Rain in sheets
fills famished soil.
Cut grass runs downhill.

It's humid, the sun is out;
the devil's beating his wife.

. . .

Soon a woodpecker resumes
its drumming
while koi come up for lunch.
Morning glories
have gone rogue in purple,
pink & blue
strangling loose rails.

run

part one

copper scales over sinew, no way not to miss you,
i swear to christ i'm psychic
in the wake of those 3:00 AM words,
i have to do this alone,
moon vines with lanced flesh
let bloodied petals go
to a fidgety disposition that's never still (be still),
to a pool room
in sync with withdrawal instincts, los angeles sex,
released today through cart-wheeling fog,
past shotgun houses & big drug dealers going green,
the smell of gullible jasmine, an expensive paradise,
tucked behind fields glittering like pirate coins,
sidewalk blues, deep like secrets, loud as birth, driving
away,
proving pisces are soothsayers
deciding the heart is a foolish child,

a fairytale motorcar, fuzzy dice, the stereo,
going to a wedding followed by waltzes
failing to flare over rotted floorboards,
minerva's prerogative,
her painful association
between a divorce & this cramped apartment
leads to the need for a violent downtown midnight,

rise bell-bottomed tinker bell in too-big sunglasses,
grandchild too good to slow down,
rising without coordinates, steering by jackson, mississippi
voodoo,
dismissing nietzsche's way around man murdering god's wonder
to altars hugged by battered arms,
far away from a thaloc, her mate

vast as faith,
always fresh as turned earth,
genuine, wet mouth whispering *we aren't damned.*

part two

one man hounded vanity, wanted worship, flipped-off jesus,
knowing better having misbehaved, one of virginia's babies
becoming a broken record spinning mad,
refusing surrender, a cut-out, brilliant cancer, rampantly
sleepless,

  slitting cupid's throat, inked by a flaming bird, whistling delta
                blues,
       creating shiny words with latin,
     not the mash-up of a runaway's slang,

        tossing out the choked scarecrow,
   racing against passing out, thoughts about being bound
               to the south,
      utopia's joke, greed, what if i don't
        know how to love,
     black keys scattered, scampering off

harmonics are always an emotional oil spill, sorrow's tempo,
tuned by mechanics
who also hock crotches at street corners, a devil-about-town,
the ability to cripple dancing, cancel last call, selling better than
religion,
hashing out procrastination, the reality of settling down,
relocating to the coast with a gentle tide

. . .

in a pub of grumpy culture,
perched beside sirens, a golfer,
& vain brother,
an attempt to move on sputters,
then suddenly: snatched from playing games
with girls easy to come by,
a better woman comes in

tripping a boy with feelings, by the ache of distance,
dipping into the wellspring of a second chance,
cradling the prospect of our nights beginning now,
her: the only moment like it was before

part three

smart strippers
make husbands forget their fat wives,
brawling between a guy's strength & his, *screw offs*,
she croons
from this, *this*,
this language of detachment, classic novels,
a beautiful waste of time, poetry slurred not spoken,
not e. e. cummings' "bud of the bud,"

indirect linguistics coming up short of containing it
all,
its nucleus loose,
a malaise of character,
a desire to seduce excuses, second guesses, apathy,
that sound of strange
the rain pings out
on tin roofs

. . .

polished third eye,
prayers to messiahs
wearing tweed & lightning
locked behind open doors
no longer arizona-lost,
scuffling ahead without disciples,
without discipline, sleeping naked,

> reminding a sinner
> home is home
> even alone,

at sunup there's us,
ready to forgive & forge ahead with vodka,
in your cynosure there's your
penchant to make us
soaring criminals, destroying worlds,
pulling down panties with entropy,
me keeping this unclaimed house key,
never growing old,
i don't want this life

Judas Noose Tavern

I eagerly wander beside William Faulkner,
off to have laughs and a drink.
Two gents together at the Judas Noose Tavern
where all sons of Bacchus meet.

We enter, *dear music!*
The quintet merges with Miles Davis.
I salute his horn with Southern Comfort,
certain this golden pub will sustain us.

My cuffs pressed, shoes buffed to a shine,
while sitting cocky there came a lady.
A succubus, a curse, a sexy suicide,
I heard earlier she'd emptied Bukowski.

Her violin fingers, possessing gray eyes,
Lilith is lithe and sultry.
She steals my thinking with rum-laden kisses,
pitting my vanity against me.

Damn her, that charm and articulate wit,
she winds a chain 'round my wrist.
Mirrors tarnish, walls grow mold,
and a gloom creeps over our tryst.

She saunters off and robs the light,
this air thickens, smelling sour.
I realize the bottle now drinks me,
and apathy begins to flower.

I can't stand and the exit is too far away.
I am another vagrant in a vacuous land.
Before I can panic she comes back
and gently holds my hand.

To Hell with Hell! Good riddance, God!
The barmaid quotes Baudelaire.
She sits by my side and whispers, *I lied,*
while I weep drunk into her hair.

A Mythical Angelica

The absence of photos
binds me to a war-torn fortune teller.
She hid needles
in her studded waistband.
Our matinee
was too short.

She played piano
to see that we
shirked what's out there.
An impetuous talk show
went on
in the background
ignored.

Now her feet travel Africa.
Plains have choked
our Southern fancy.
Another lover
will walk on baked earth.

Macerated veins,
like old wallpaper,
fold over my heart.

launching

on the edge of new life, our nexus,
a lucky pair making plans out of limbo,
there is silence.
worrying the fates will intercede with cruelty,
she barely speaks.
i do not wear it well.

on our fringes there's no mystery.
the battle is that pretty face
twisted by tears and abandonment.
herculean grief starts here.
zeus' suggestions stoke our appetite,
half divine, not quite
making our affection a blessing.

a road has stolen her closeness to me.
the door is flung open
with nothing outside but
a humid afternoon.

the smaller vices, the nights glittering
with words that make her feel radiant
are strained.
our sex is on the verge
of passing into death.

Crush

On this slow day
I'm lingering
on thoughts of you.

You are the catalyst
and the razor,
the haunting
I can't remember.

Three for the Going Again

part one

The night took down
its azure complexion
as she swore me off.
I hear those who kissed me before
scoff all the Confederacy
she fits.

My sweet Mason-Dixon
cinches her belt
with a Mother Mary buckle.
Be brave, tug together
your sacred, rarely-worn
weathered jacket.
Leave this gambler with
no good hand.

part two

Why am I doing this?

Because I'm yours, because
the spectators
are telling scary stories,
because this January blizzard
has locked me away
from relief.

She is Heloise
without a neutered Abelard
whining.
She gave up Petrarch
so Laura

will lose nothing having
given up
his love letters.

part three

I cannot cry
over discontent
within my liver,
kidneys,
my vacant iris.

I plague her.
I have pushed
my sad darling
to miss these hips,
to bounce between hotels
along illicit trade routes.

I am a worn out
recliner she kept
but never sat.

Skim your tear-wet paws
over the braille
of my wrists.
Old reflections
speak to me
in dreams,
She is the only witness.

driven myth's foreword

thoughts of folding
are folded up,
then discarded
like bad directions.

clinging to synaptic trinkets,
her photos are cherished
in a cellular phone.
rose: raised sideways on an island,
her appaloosa waits
with a tangled mane.

a mourning walk
to a motel
on the ugliest side of athens;
his feet where hers
once were.

. . .

tomorrow:

the bronx, banjos, metacarpals
and *life—*

intestines healing, musculature
at ease, sleeping.
she saunters beyond speakeasies
closed to those in a cotton dress
and little else.
walking
farther away from anxiety,
now
dangling

like
turning
leaves.

it is as it is,
the story of a lady
who ran fast, singing etta james,
riding a phagocyte
into quilts fashioned
by a feisty grandmother.
there the girl is rediscovered.

if it is the she before:
go back to that
violet-strewn towpath. (remember?)
forget horrible months
shot
with abandonment
missing loose, shoulder-length hair,
a tart lower lip
and ochre paints from egypt.

it's you.
the exotic music
licking necks, the small-of-backs
and belly buttons.

. . .

spring:

one mother stares from a harbor,
stooped
on the west coast.
be not sad.

with recumbent pink toenails
the child flies east
wearing a tiny diamond
nose ring.

Coffee House Layouts

Chai is a thick brand of
bourgeoisie snot.
Track lighting
throws itself around sticky.
Art students with running mascara
take a booth by the unisex bathroom.

They are caricatures.
Smokers cling outside
every entrance.
Standing close in the cold
and sometimes laughing,
babes enjoy cloves and cappuccino.

Ascension, First Floor Up

A girl sneaks into that comfortable
middle-space
in every bed
where she's learned
not to share the covers.

There were bad deeds,
and once before
they cast whole shadows
that seem less opaque tonight.
Now they're gossamer wind
across a white,
closed door.

An owl calls, lifts off
and bursts into the particles
of perfect dreams.

. . .

The knees of these jeans
suffer spreading patches
as their chemistry corrodes. Even so,
a vineyard is woven across my torso,
the wine of a god's patience
pressed between heartbeats.
A murmuring third *thump*
injects one breath
of hopeful resignation.
Fingers itch for the turn
of the ignition.

A giant toddler with tattoos
and broken eyes. It's the draw.
*Broken—she dances for your
broken eyes.*
Savannah's road beers
fail to heal the lack
of standing still.

Getting home from Tupelo
we're free from the long road.
Let me fetch your guitar.

A harmonica blows
from the street below.
Languishing, *Sketches of Spain*
lingers here.

. . .

I don't know how this story goes,
how pages fit together;
this place, the secret:

*I am
because you are.*

It is you, this rose's
open mouth.
A blossom,
single in its yellow vase,
casting only sunlight
where a shadow
should be.

In the imagination,
without a map,
a pair is jammed up proper,
smoking Lucky Strikes,
rocking an Oldsmobile 442.

Colors of the Parrish, Sex and Essence

This canvas requires a carnival,
the sound of an evening ocean,
a glen only satyrs know.

Brushstrokes convince landscapes
to rise, breach,
capture an eclipse of form
and function, a maple leaf adrift,
waning light in mid-shift.

I don't enjoy my day as a Monet.
This is not Waterhouse
watching Ophelia drown.
The world has had its Parrish
with fairies,
and lantern-carrying clowns.

I choose blue. Curves of it
over a previous gray start.
What better hue
to see through than blue?
The impeccable sky,
this brooding mood, June's winking dew,
it's mine and yours
and blue.

Mine are sirens lingering in a frame.
They wink, cajole and coo.
Slinking ladies
who drink from my fingers
always smiling for you.

Waiting

part one

Twilight is drawn out,
bed sheets made up, one sits
and music plays unheard.
Athena's recollection is that
I am the last
dying
Stonewall Jackson.

Too skinny, twitchy,
these limbs bear the fragrance of bareness.
Her footsteps zig-zag the South
like outlaws
with little time left.

Devotion is the chariot, the disappointment,
the long walk to nowhere
infested with shadows.
A young lady takes her father's
thievery of presence
       up
          to her bosom.

part two

*So we snip off the ends and beginnings, the old friendships
and new hangers-on. I am cinders
between your hands held in prayer. We are in the highest
boughs.*

. . .

I am not the forest where great men go
to hunt deer.
I am not the field where pheasant are
flushed out and shot.
I am not the jagged peak
where warriors die and ascend.

She is the cellist's taunt thighs
around my stout resonance.
Once jazz club-possessed,
thrice tossed farther away.

I claim the prize
of satisfying
her resolution.

part three

We are water nymphs unkissed, unwanted,
untouched,
too disconnected to deliver
one good drowning.

We are falling ions
sidestepping earth's droll traffic.
We are spared the compromise
of moving-in
with a prattling distraction.

We would say to them:
You are a tourist.
I am bored with this.

Lie naked with me, warped,
wrapped up like wet towels.
We are not scuffed up old shoes.
Rest now, you,
sweet Saturday-morning—
flat-of-the-tongue.

Nightless Dreams

part one

(01/15/03)

Tell a tale and stop the clock.
Wind me down like a pocket watch.
Night spreads out
a heavy chill.
The sandman is a fickle bastard.

part two

(04/14/04)

Wicked stars
howl in choirs.
I am throbbing. Slumber
doesn't lumber in
so easy.

part three

(10/26/04)

Enveloped by life,
giving better, desperately generous,
still cuckolded by Karma.

part four

(03/12/05)

There is more to little deaths.
Another chapter on your long legs,
folklore of an orgasm to come
flares the bloodstream.

part five

(05/16/06)

We can hide ourselves
in the Amazon
tucked behind knots in strong trees.
It's a comforting thought.

blackberries & blue *morpho didius*

backed by a striking falsetto,
the room is set
for blue *morpho didius*,
wings out.
(a cobalt coming of age
with two spent at its ending.)

> notes scurry to the corners of this space.
> sad/redemptive songs
> ring out in chorus:
> how can lovers
> be both fixed
> & in flux?

blackberries are cold in a bowl
off the right hand side
of my leather chair.
i feel old. joints pop
in weary getting-up warfare.
i know that my clock
ticks
    off-kilter
        these days.

> suddenly,
> a handful of bursting fruit!
> the taste of her mouth.
> the feel of her pierced nipples
> comes to me the morning after.
> our consciousness is
> one honeycomb
> breathing with secrets.
> nature's wet conduit
> collects in the cups
> behind my knees.

worshiping the real invisible,
hot hymns drip off the chin
beneath perfect teeth.
the self is left:
the death/learning/lesson(s)
that spans our room's width,
it's the only purity we share.
only the concrete seeps through
my thickest veil,
                finally coming up with glimmers
                                of a strange life.
                        blue *morpho didius*
                bow at the edge of blackberry vines
                                in my mind.
                it's an image after strewn clothes
                become a bed deconstructed.
                there's middle georgia architecture
                                & odd conversations
                about coming/going home.

            bind two breaths
        quarter moon between us.
            there is nothing else.

A History

part one

In hard times the mind is absent from itself.
The abandonment
shoves a permanent edge
into the jugular's cleft.

Old Sunday come-home songs
resonate from the faith of a black woman
that promise a bosom of forgiveness
to a sorry son who refused to thrive.
In the valley is her grave, her headstone,
a long white shadow.

part two

To the wind go regrets lodged between neurons
that remember the attic, boxing gloves, and hard boards
beneath muddy shoes.
Ladies with green eyeliner look like
their gall bladder escaped
behind a blurry hindsight,
getting away from corroded livers.
A young man tells stories
from his pure history,
a subjective bitch.

part three

Oh, timid soul!
Sun-dried pulp, the flock's testimony feels false,
wadded, keeping a clear consciousness
from moving with muscle.
Palpitations beneath these
concave ivories, disbelieve,
click with a third beat
begging,
begging,
begging,
for more *amore.*

part four

Dented, duct-taped breaths rattle
and pull oxygen into a delusion.
Home – come home, homeless one. Be sweet to the barbarian
who strips off coarse wool to swoon you.

Ours will be a lifetime beside a warm hearth,
hugged by hydrangeas, set right
beneath a comforting dawn.

Our Couch

I say:

The Beats were idiots.
Kerouac drank double time
because he was lumped
in with junky friends.
Naked Lunch was only cool
because acid adults said so.
Ginsberg endures,
dying after seeing his syllables
on a marquee.

. . .

Novellas and sketch books
are strewn across our coffee table
free of home improvement magazines.
Loose papers
rise, flutter, then scatter
due to June's whisper
let in through an open
kitchen window.

A glass of forgotten water from last night
is poured out and refilled without bad spirits.
I place it iced near you
not too close to spill.
Granny's psychedelic covers
are pulled over our bare contours,
promising us *la vita nuova.*
Teeth are brushed
before reality becomes dreamy fiction.

You're not listening,
drifting and always you.
Our last shot was caught by daybreak.
Now we're romanced by these breezy
moments before Monday.
Cool, hugging cushions keep us too content,
we giving in to being lazy.
Even still, come curvier into me,
jellybean.

Neighbors seem busy
making their afternoon finale
a hurried mess.
We wove our weekend from reggae and tomato sandwiches,
getting lost again dancing naked.
You balanced your tiny feet on mine.

The Death of an Oasis

Once I shared rent
with a woman.
Eleven years later
I see the break up
from that affair;
a battle I could've handled better.

We graduated from college
and ate sushi
in a renovated railway car.
Our apartment
had a fantastic pool
with an island and waterfalls.

Trying to stay sober,
it came down to friends vs. lovers.
We split up.
Big boy problems
were packed along with socks and books.
I believe her family was relieved.

Manhood came knocking
moving out of our pad.
I loathed her cat.
I remember her favorite bands.
I broke her heart.

II. Whirling Metaphysics

A Pink Mat

She strode into the room with a pink mat,
smiling because her body
would bend back
like a serpent.

On the floor a leg is thrown
over and twists with balance to arch.
Like a lotus flower she unfolds
in a cotton dress.

The Café

Night is in a foul mood.
The café is wood-paneled and slipshod.
Leafless branches, clean phalanges,
scrape across frosted windows.

Eyes hopscotch
over the crowd.
A novice guitar player
and Jack Daniels
keep patrons warm.

Outside snow makes men quick,
run, run, newcomers shiver.
Raw noses are pressed against sleeves.
Indoors we reminisce
over estivation,
pretending to hear waves.

Orchid Incident

Evidence of a wicked man
is in this woman's bath.
Her lover's been long kicked out.
She can be seen through one window.
Condensation obscures her. A leg crests,
then stretches forward.

A bottle of rum, one orchid
on a silver tray. Shot glass
thrown back three times.
Beneath a bare bulb she hums
as Strauss conducts *Metamorphosen.*

Wound around her ankle is a green dragon tattoo.

Kingston State of Mind

part one

I slip on blue sunglasses.
Start up the car,
windows to the ground.
Beethoven buckles up shotgun.

Brunette girls in sandals
dodge shady men at the bus stop.
Traffic is slow, accommodating
my mood.

part two

I put on blue sunglasses.
Start up the car, spark an acrid clove,
windows to the ground.
Beethoven rides beside me.

Pretty girls furiously texting
stand outside a coffee shop.
Traffic is slow. Cops are busy
somewhere else.
I need to get laid.

Quartet in A Minor

A man alone in prison
hears God laughing.
Thoroughly removed below
he hears no nightingales.
The wind does not reach
this scab of tortured earth.

Tonight is his escape.
Slumber brings his family.
A mind needs no society.
The prison is a joke,
as is the laughter,
as is God.

Wednesday Evening

Jasmine tea spins with milk,
more cream between sips.
The cup occupies her nightstand.
None of these pillows match.

A painting of anorexic suffering
hangs sideways.
We in this condition
are warped.

Midnight Alley Wolves

There's a 3:00 AM bleakness
to some people.
They are ghosts
paying homage
to a dead city.

Disheveled, furtive,
traveling
outside daylight's periphery,
the pavement
devours their memory.

The Small Now and Then

You're such a business woman now.
I'm the one with tattoos and earrings,
writing without a shirt on.
You're ironing
pant suits on Saturday night.

Unburdened

Wisteria winds its way
up the colonnades
of my family's ancient home.
Easing past noon
I'm lost
in my mind here
clearly with her.

I want to think on
our émigré status.
She hears my heartbeat.
Great-uncle's roses
unfurl.

Across the street
bells ring hymns.
Now they toll six.
The bells are innocuous,
we expect no borrowed time.

Man Ignored

He preens for no reason.
Age is an asshole of a bedfellow.
Happy hours pass their elasticity.
Bar stools lose their glamour.

Beauty dies,
becoming sullen and dull.
As time slides
the less people care.

Poem

A tricycle leans
under the cedar tree.
Motown is playing on vinyl.
These houses don't seem
so close together.

Little has changed
here on the green steps.
Next door a woman brings down laundry.
There is no traffic, no strangers,
a fence between us and the asylum.

Brunch

The waitress is too chipper.
She knows my wife somehow.
Soccer rushes by on one television
while another shows stock cars.

The hedges are cut
in rectangles.
The parking lot is clogged
with hybrid cars
that look like Easter eggs.

Nostalgia

Nostalgia is ruinous,
the slow death of better days.
Some kind of undigested glory
for lepers,
to those who don't love it
it's a specious tale told by drunks.

In an Afternoon

The two of us in bed,
a nap after wine and piano,
we're busy whispering,
stomachs growling,
two heads are hidden under sheets
so our friends won't call.

I love this day,
these lazy afternoons,
your pink toenails,
your eyelashes.

Most of all,
you.

porcelain trees

porcelain trees
glow frozen in some eastern
morning or evening
it's unmoving
deaf
a soft facade
the imperfections
of authenticity aren't included
few can enjoy it
stars will not fall
birds do not call

Hammock

Eyes closed, leaves tickle each other,
wind swimming between them.
There's the school bus,
a lawnmower,
two dogs barking
at nothing.

Thinking in an Argument

Creamer reacts and disappears
in a plume.
The cloud
becomes swirls
which spread out as threads,
leaving coffee
less itself than before.

My skin is thin as onion skin
and I don't know
what you want to hear.

Inclined

Look upon me,
the moody alchemy
of a jagged man.

You ought to know
my heart is a harlot.

Epiphany

Creativity is incivility,
a thorn, unapologetic,
the compassionate ransom note.

Do not envy
this nightly fight
with ecstasy.

Written During a Seminar

I awoke untied from earth.
Silence is tenuous at 6:00 AM.
Children are louder
than garbage men.

My drive to the office
is a brick-to-the-brain.
Work is there
but I am a stone.

Half listening
to the business of business,
it's lost.

Heretics

Heretics
are forged
from logical
copulation
with faith.

Pissed off good men,
beautiful, altered,

scarred,

are busy preparing
the next best reason
to hang on.

Falling South

Fall comes down quick
like an excited teenager.
Leaves are red only seconds.
Hills are blown naked.

A speed bump
of soft breezes
buffers December.
There is little symmetry
in the South.

Dogwoods

Dogwoods sway
leafless this evening
holding Wang Wei's missing branch.
It's cold now.

A match and smoke,
hot spots wink
in hearths.
Those dogwoods are
ladies reaching towards November.

Three Nights at the Plantation

At eleven years old
my great-aunt
gave me coffee.
Staying overnight
I slept on the screened porch,
coddled in that gentle dark.
Waking, breakfast,
it felt like the life
of a prince.

Extracurricular criminals
we plotted on leather couches,
smoked where Civil War
soldiers once stood.
An unmentionable evening
made from semi-automatic weapons
and Maker's Mark.

A blue lady filters through,
then saunters across
the room. Dead come here.
A house breathing,
the unfeeling brick
speaks at night.
Ghosts watch us sleep
and whisper
gibberish.

Appalachian Exile

part one

The gravel over old roads
calls beneath cars
with voices
like white noise.

All summer, through trees, past cattle,
farther than the
heady smell of farmland
an open window lets in a ladybug.

Kudzu frames and haloes
signs and telephone poles.
Thick, spinning clouds of gnats await
inattentive citizens
to invade their ears, nose, and mouth.

Along the creek bed,
chest bare to the elements,
a man looks at crawdads
scuttling under rocks.

Shadows shield nervous fish
from crushing beaks.
Exposed roots
reach through soil
like gnarled fingers.

The pines, with a handshake,
kindly meet water.
Robins and whippoorwills modulate
from branches,
twittering in a stand-off.

Waves of katydids
hidden in the brittle ground
speak with two sonorous notes.
Beyond low mountains
he is caught by this spot.
The evening begins to whisper in
and moss stretches
out as a blanket.

part two

Alone, his car coasts along,
beaten by branches.
Past a house abandoned,
there are no hands left
to pick blackberries.

Hearth and half-chimney
jut up like the home's tombstone.
Roof, front porch, shutters
all devoured by the earth.

Above brambles
kudzu smothers
a telephone pole.
Moving forward,
mountains begin to stand taller.

Brought here by his father
he returns as a man
having spent too long
in the city.

Deeper still, farther away
tall weeds
lead to a fertile cathedral.
Whippoorwills alight
trees growing closer together.

Ghosts of other
loners, like the heat, wave.
Chest bare, stomach
and buttocks exposed,
he bravely dances in the sun.
Into a swimming hole
long legs leap, body
washed by real water.

Loose roots
like gnarled fingers
reach past soil into this river.
Moss-slick rocks
now disturbed
cast silt around him.

Floating, deserted, happy,
he is a wren, this cold river,
a sleeping mountain lion.

Road to the Coast

Car already rolling, wife and I leave.
The local scene dissolves.
Piggly Wiggly fades away
and day becomes bluer still
driving south.

We kiss at red lights.
Georgia is a blur.
Alabama cities
called Cantonment, Flomaton and Opelika
separate budding ghost towns
full of lightning-struck trees.

The Lost Highway plays itself out
and Hank Williams Sr. sings.
Florida feels like youth
and we are part of its waters.

Feet planted in the dunes,
she holds my pinky finger
while dolphins make children squeal,
looping in June.

The Huddle House

A balding man
with an incredible wart
on his crown
talks about lazy plumbers.
His wife twirls a keychain
with dice clinging to it.
One kid with no shirt
throttles the gumball machine.

Coffee tastes like a dirty fist.
The barstools are filled
with travelers in denim.
A film coats the very air,
but these waitresses shut up,
leave you alone,
allowing everyone
to quietly follow traffic.

On the Last Wild Edge

Sunset, back wet from hard work,
hands raw from shovels,
firewood stands in clean stacks
by the back door.
A hawk sits on telephone wire
watching cut fields.

Men and women retire indoors.
Orange is smeared
behind mountains bursting
at the seams. Trees
are an unkempt mane.
It's a curved, unbroken line
where bears sleep in winter.

With so much rain
the view has a gauzy sheen.
Rugged life is in the walls
of small homes on the edge.
The quiet spirits a man away
witnessing natural decay.

Never misplaced or confused
the bones and blood are from this earth,
these flowers, the crops.

Saturday Night in Athens

Autos are boarded then dissolve.
Painted faces and Polo shirts,
couples are cabbed together.

Small parties primp and flirt
with oyster-fed anxiety.
Their voices are exaggerated,
accepting, and tipsy.

They come, leave, then come again.
All the same, swooning on freedom,
sliding towards 1:00 AM.

I lean, loaf, and feel old
from this second story window.
Staring off, sober,
I'm a voyeur
watching for bluesy women.

The Civil War and Whores

There were Civil War generals
who had hookers and booze
in their ranks.

Prostitutes capitalized
on young, brazen men
already romanced by valkyries.

View from My Office

Wildflowers stand
in untouched crevices.
Lawnmowers couldn't slice
through rock.
Some violet sprigs survived.

Root-cracked parking lots
prove how man is beaten.
Little towns don't
wear time well.
Everything green outgrows us.

One train every three days,
a cemetery sits across those old tracks.
Tombstones lean in shambles
like crooked teeth.
Moss consumes them,
blanketing the forgotten.

Robins zip and bob.
Muscadine vines bear fruit.

Remember Lakeside Manor

Lemonade stains a hardwood floor.
Children are out of school.
The brave wisely avoid snakes.

Boyhood is tragically perfect.

Floating face up,
calm is between youth and open air.
Leaves break apart the veil.

I Saw the Klan Today

Morning headed to Bell's,
Klansmen haunted the courthouse.
I was eight.
Virginia seethed,
Some folks like to live ugly.

Her almond knuckles
pale on the steering wheel,
our car sped up.
She had wild eyes
on those violent phantoms.
In wedding white,
faces tight
behind a bed sheet,
they were chanting.

Virginia patted my knee,
Don't even look at 'em, baby.
At home I slept in her lap.
She hummed "Go Tell It on the Mountain,"
praying I would grow into a man
who witnessed wrong
and became a blade against it.

My mahogany mother
squeezed me, smoothed my hair,
sad at the state
of our world.

Cold Rain

Sleet is doused down
like chicken feed.
Guys leave their wives
in warm vehicles
to do what men do in Home Depot.

One truck has a broken heater,
the condensation too thick
to see inside.
A taillight is broken, doors two-toned,
bumper sticker reads, *The South Shall Rise Again!*
And do what?

On a Train

Train-traveling was a cabaret.
Buildings and lights smeared
as an infant fussed.
From my seat, one row up,
a Nefertiti in blue jeans
read a book.

Near the rear a man, lost,
stared out with tired, yellow eyes.
Another couple made out,
moving hands beneath a checkered blanket.
I passed them,
swaying like a drunkard
to the smoking car.

The ride rushed me towards a girl.
Three days later we wept
on the same platform
with desperate goodbyes.

Ticket turned in again,
my suitcase was taken
up the stairs.
Like the strongest parent,
that Appalachian Express
rocked me back to Georgia.

Sunday Chaconne

Drinking absinthe
outside the Vortex
my friend buys lunch.
Sinatra sings in a passing car
as pink hair, street preachers,
and we two lucid revelers
step on
the same sidewalk.

Barely brushing the ground
traveling asphalt tributaries
trees thin,
museums rise up,
stone carves itself into forms.
Graffiti blurs into an urban Pollock.
Shop windows
warp our reflections.

Atlanta concrete greets us;
her face, many faces.
Skyscrapers lose us
among anthropology students.
Homeless squatting with Styrofoam cups
don't accost us.

We're happily ambivalent,
oozing around eye contact,
invisible;
a speck in the sea of this city.

Crowds hush,
air shimmers,
pigeons burst
upward.

There are Hours

This is havoc,
a red-splattered cheek,
change in sunlight.

My stance is aloof, distracted,
right foot dragging
from watching my father limp
with a fake hip.

As a child I picked up his pill box,
his money clip, that carnal eye.
He shook me
because of my coming broken heart.

There is choice, then the reality of bloodlines,
of recurring men,
of one wolf giving way
to an animal his brood
but sharper, better at being feral, a scourge.
Pop's lectures were lost,
incinerated on my spirit.

He told me: *What cannot be released*
will stalk
and mangle another life.

I hold no rose in lakeside grasses.
In my arms there is no basket
of intimacy unfulfilled.
No scripture whispers in my twisted ear.

How does a cloistered man,
with a gaping wound,
dismiss his bleeding, his gushing?
In this labyrinth
I can't find the leading thread out.
I am Minos and his gluttonous son.

. . .

A lady gives me a volley of crushing anchors.
Love is spindled only in one artery.
Through churning valves
I allow a single set of platelets.
This is a leak of what was
but never was. (Us.)
Stone is the softest aorta.

I cannot go on eclipsed.
I am more than that silver peeking.
I'm the soothing ring behind what's lonely
only because of stabbing fate.
Right now my pretty girl
drives fast out-of-state.

Enter melancholy cinders!
I eat fists of pomegranate
for more time in Hades;
quiet, in the bowels,
beneath this constant barrage.
Languishing among shades, forgetting,
I will be no one.

The trees, plantation songs,
those goddamned morning glories
flutter above me

like looting butterflies
whose wings move so loudly
better sense screams in vain.
In vain those angels exhausted point away from Styx,
begging, knowing I still hear them.

Sing aloud "Salve Regina."
I am me.
I'm content to be marked a libertine
welcoming another messy orgasm as a swan
to experience virgins.
New breasts avert the vision of one girl.

Run me from her.
In a wheelbarrow carry my clattering bones to
Lexington's empty church house.

Gas Station Purgatory

People drone into tiny phones.
Their mouths are ragged metal
that clangs
while I'm standing in line.
I'm deaf to everything else
but that clanging
clamoring in.

Their ruckus is a jumble of nonsense
pilfered from some relative,
friend, TV show.
Sartre's right
about other people.

This gas station is necessary.
I am stuck,
strangled by lottery tickets.
Beef jerky looks lethal.
There's a rack of legal
speed for the graveyard shift.
That clanging
is a test.

Blues Solo

Bloodshot on a moon-hung highway,
I wear my soul like a chore.
This solid '67 Impala
rolls with mellow wheels,
and hauls me home to Crawford.
I can't seem to shake the line,
Ain't nobody's fault but mine.

I feel like a prophet with smoke in his eyes,
seeing rhyme that burns like brimstone.
It's the spell of her love letters
on the back seat
beneath John Lee Hooker's guitar.
I am bewitched. I have come unstitched.
A rosary swings
from the rearview mirror.

Nighttime is a shade of day; it passes.
This isn't The Blues Café in Smyrna
where I read John Agard poems
while my last romance got a headstone.
Sitting there I first heard the line,
Ain't nobody's fault but mine.

This lady says she'll forgive me,
inviting these bones back for safe keeping.
Car grumbling, trembling apart,
trees eat into my periphery.
For months this man
has been a wasteland.
I haven't shaved in five days,
and a shower wouldn't kill me.

Diaphanous

A diaphanous skin covers nettles
to neon signs.
Its fingers
touch the nape of my neck.
Gravediggers must pray for
our longevity until first thaw.
I live here, sitting under its weight,
a weekend with nowhere to be.

How Far into the Tumultuous Night

A staggering amount of hours
are spent staring off.
From bed I wonder
why I'm awake exactly on the hour
as if the hour
wouldn't arrive
if I weren't there.

Eyes are open in the farthest corner.
Time watches my discomfort.
Silence is screaming
I can't stand.
Knees tucked up into my chest,
light will come like a hangover.
Roosters crow too soon.

Spring Dancing

Up, up! Slip back, swoon,
come apart w/ me
and toddle along.

I'll take you over a tombstone,
throw back, and howl
at the moon.

I'll baptize, sanctify,
you, us, in dew.
Our wishes
are for freedom.

Drink up!
Swim to me,
sweet somersault girl.
We two evening dwellers
are spinning
drunk on stars.

Indian-sitting in the ocean,
we breathe Destiny
and radiate keepsakes.

Darling kitten paws,
we'll give God
great licorice kisses
for breakfast.

my buddhist beginning

little blue marble,
locked in great-grandmother's
fragrant tin,
    i found you
    poured out in apples.
    you there at my buddha's feet.

how funny
that i found you
in that
old bronze box,
    you looking
    so young and rescued.

i'll discuss
your finer points
often on my journey,
keeping you
in a desk drawer.
    i'll discover you
    tomorrow
    and we'll
    read this poem together.

Daydreams & Dime Bags

Herman Melville is speaking to
royalty in New England.
I'm in the crowd,
head taller than everyone else,
staring at his blizzard of a beard.
I can't hear what he's saying.

It's a dangerous place to be
trapped,
pacing,
scrabbling to be better.
[Doing good
because being good's
too hard.]

. . .

Sunflowers slip open
and into something more corruptible.
With them
wandering jew and alyssum
sprawl naked, entangled.

Out there, against the glass,
bluebirds crash into their reflection.

Dream Casting

On the backs of pine beetles
burrowed beneath dense
tree bark
this journey is hidden.

. . .

The bedroom window's hairline cracks
turn streetlights into muted prisms.
In the parking lot below,
talk of pancakes and bar fights.
I'm somewhere between it
and sleep, finally drifting off.

Next morning hands
cupped around coffee, I sit
a fresh persona.
Bare feet feel alive
on this hardwood floor.
Dust sparkles,
sifts, and settles.

Six Chapters of Swerve

part one

Friday: Patsy Cline plays
on a red Corsa's radio:
I go walkin' after midnight.
Roaring around loose gravel turns,
whipping by dark shanties,
I'm headed to a honky-tonk in Bethlehem.

Last week's turmoil is tossed out
and flares up
like a discarded cigarette.

part two

2:00 AM demands
my undivided attention.
The evening brings wraiths
and I whittle ghouls into phrase.

Boredom,
writing a line, maybe two,
in the eye of this typhoid fever
I feel my ill-healed wounds.
Does evening hear me?

Yes.

Like gypsy neurons
thoughts of salvation
and self-satisfaction argue
through loose association.
This is quiet too deep.
There is no resignation.

part three

Saturday:
Morning is an awkward nap.
I'm nervous, tired,
trying to shine like chrome.
Trash burning smells too strong.
Noise is a tearing bear claw.
It's one more, another walk out
into mist.

part four

Noon is a humid sheen
graced by geraniums.
Craving focus I mend mother's lawn.
Weeds are pulled with callused hands.
Heat crawls across flesh in sweat,
singeing shoulders.

Go, go, go!
With machines and bent back
I retaliate against the taste
of gun metal.

Deep breaths can't catch
a pulse outside natural fact.
All I can do is choose to move.
This labor delays the
attraction to chaos.

part five

Sunday:
Excessive energy is spent
pensive, stressed already
about another uninvited
week of calamity.

Panic is a midnight snack.
Wait.
One blink, a moody shift
and I'm Uncle Remus
in his reading chair;
one cool glass of water.
There's no pressure.

Protection, this mnemonic smoke screen
is a parlor trick. I know
it isn't going to be okay.

part six

Monday: An unfriendly 4:34 AM.
It's late again.
Insomnia says
more time will make a difference.

If you're up,
idling, my Corsa's
doors are open.
Forget the lack of dreams
that this night is.

Get in!
We will drive, listen to Patsy Cline,
and drift
beside a ribbon
of bending willows.

An Affair of Fireflies

During this downpour
a capricious waltz
begins between fireflies and lightning.

Dozens of these Peaseblossoms
twinkle in response to flares.
The air sizzles.

Insects and blinding splinters
kiss the same sky,
oblivious to human interpretation.

The storm retreats
and clearing wind
snuffs out the last dark cloud.

In the calm
stars flicker on
and fireflies fall for the cosmos.

fleeting

rain argues with day's end

vacant corners cast in secrecy
coaxing us from the holiday crowd
and cake

she tastes like kiwi
an indulgence
her christmas gift

no witnesses
to our currents of want
that compress and expand

this escape
is a precarious continent
it's a loss of control

thunder moves the furniture

a late poem to *blue train*

blueberry stains
on my fingertips
are a distraction.
the refrigerator whirs,
filling this void.

. . .

cigarettes and heroin didn't soothe
him as blue train *kicked up dust*

rain smells of marmalade
through a peeling screen door.

out in it, i'm propped up by cassiopeia.
sucking breaths, cool nightshade,
give praise to the resting sun.

black-eyed susans
grow in merciless tendrils.
tree frogs trill from maples.

it was a spider

burgundy flora is placed
and eight legs race
from it
across the oak table
a snow-white spider
the second in three days
replaces the first one
i killed

number two is hiding
in a bundle of coxscomb
the ghost of a crystal spinner
at buddha's feet
i am a reed
a puff of air

Hands Dappled with Honey

Hands dappled with honey,
held palm-to-palm,
bless ancient, leaping throngs.
Club Deus ex Machina
is open to dicey souls,
Nietzsche's dancing stars.

. . .

Quail whorl through first chill.
The fowl hide, panic, then warbling
are shot.

Men the color of trees
send out dogs.

Grasses play a dirge.

The Tragedy of Waiting Helen

New day with a poor man's Achilles
still living but defeated, telling stories
of a Helen tortured by Troy, worshiped by criminals,
beauty a tragic flower where thugs beat their wives.

A solitary note almost broken by old men,
Helen played, was cast off over deserts and wet winters,
pale arms thrown open in Africa, jailed
spreading dread-locked virtue.

There is dark water over her. Paris and Hector
are hyenas at the bank of her inferno
snapping, snickering, snarling to have
the softness left of her in their guts.

Ravens crowd branches, silent,
waiting above such noisy scoundrels.
A piano plays in that deep. Guitar strings, battered veins
beneath such a fragile patina.

Little Girl Saint only half-martyred,
tossed back without transcendence. No honors, no prayers,
no candles but that howling blue flame
cupped over her mouth.
No one has launched a paper armada for her soul.

Lunar Love's Wanting

Beneath an asymmetrical moon
we are Orpheus & Eurydice
successfully undead,
naked, carnal
on the banks
of Averno.
This union dares up
the need for a dark alley.

Forehead-to-forehead,
we are impervious.
On a back-arched axis
our Aristophanes' halves
congeal.
Orion aside that pitted disk,
they stand guard
& bear witness.

Resurgence

Taking turns to dig ancients out,
Hank Mobley records get shuffled
with Kerouac's drunken haikus
and Nat King Cole's "Route 66."

Discolored cardboard,
unsellable a decade ago,
now redeems itself.

Real dervishes keep a table spinning
to dance while they decide
Ray LaMontagne
sounds like a thoughtful winter.

Before Nirvana, Grieg

Before Nirvana, Grieg
crowned the Mountain King.
His corridors, adopted by grunge
and old trolls,
walked one to suicide.
Rock's maudlin blonde
got shot-out pathetic
in the guesthouse.

Peer wouldn't wear
the same rotten crown,
his head against Solveig's bosom.
Live at Reading pauses
to honor Aase's suite death.
Legions light funeral pyres.

Violins mourn the quasi-prophet,
family absent and everywhere.
The last tone,
a cello far from Norway,
ripples through Seattle
with desert sands
and Bedouin kisses.

The Universe Throws Darts

An arroyo is beneath me
thick with mist like liquid wool.
Sky full of keyholes, the deceased
slide down in invisible crowds
to hover, swoop, then launch themselves
over mortal walls
joining those still breathing, smelling like coffee,
in a bakery at 5:00 AM.

. . .

Romance redesigned epiphany:
Abandon quills and soliloquy
for a good brawl and bare words!
Rely on water. Take dates to the riverbank
where people are given a pass, reborn,
freed through *l'eau de la vie.*

. . .

Quarks and black holes, alternate dimensions,
here are real as stone;
mother's favorite misfits.
Their math and mountains aren't ours.
We are intentionally held at the moon.
Evolution is locked away, selfish, in a foreign jungle,
unyielding.

. . .

Guarded by a bitter aunt, a widow
miserable she woke up,
there is a place for unlived dreams,
for 8-track players and typewriters,
for the last Atari on our ashy surface.

Snapshots from Line of Sight

part one

Wheat splits and sways.
Wind is hard on stalks.
Sun pours down
on everyone.

Men curse their wives
who keep them
from cards and beer.
Pall Malls are spit out with a pinch.

part two

Nights are a long ache.
Bored stars, moon, no room to move.
Shelves slanted.

The desk is a strange friend.
Soon gray light seeps in, a bad joke.
Numb in a daylong dream state.

part three

Dead leaves
drift down warped stairs.
Chicks peck for bugs
in the cold.
Trees come up a slope,
past a pile of iron, tires,
and coils.

part four

The truth is small,
a chirp
from a bird
on a branch.

Out in the yard
the talk of it
is lost on me.
A plan too hard
to walk.

part five

Love isn't a chore.
Heart is simple.
Little words are best.

We Heave Up Like the Night

It's snowing, our reflections stained,
captured in clean puddles.
We came down tonight
like resurrected clerics
who followed Hypnos
above city lights to skip time.
Physics bends as we have seconds slow.
Strangers are left to window shop.

"A Desdemona Nocturne," " The New L.A. Woman,"
she's singing like Nina Simone.
Sashaying conspiracy of lyrics and lace,
the lady rattles my teeth.
Who we were has been misplaced.
The sticky fusion fuels
our need to be alone.

So alive, compressed through my spine,
she becomes home, candlelight,
anguish,
velvet midnight,
the early morning hard love
and smallest mouth.
Palms held out with threaded fingers,
we hear the vapid mob.

The Fifth Movement

intro

Morpheus: *Moonlight opens*
a pale autumn sky,
a strange, inviting glow.

With hawk's wings
I trickle down in diamonds,
over angry Artemis and snow.

part one

The cosmos comes wrapped in a tantrum;
a squalling, flailing,
spoiled child sliding through eons
to create phenomena and failure.
All of it, clarinets to coworkers,
a single, outward motion.

A marvelous biological cauldron: You.

You are perpetual
and we are monks chanting over taxi drivers
as Minerva gathers her flock.

Step lightly. Now shine brash and brightly.
This Transfiguration is jazzed
up by Cannonball Adderley.

part two

Let stress assuage for an evening
you banker, you Russian bread maker,
you, the strong father.
Dreamy spires penetrate wakeful smog,
shearing back nightmares of conflict.

Fall asleep slump-shouldered pilgrims.
Swing into my void.

part three

Coming-of-age goes on too long.
Our youth surfs,
sliding along myelin sheaths
to bring back innocence in a bell jar.

Once it's bashed open
a launching of joyful nymphs
snatch back gilded days,
naive days, reliving
philosophy and exquisite trysts.

Chica bonita, lament no more
for Rodin is for all time in the same stone
so common man
can tend to his common tasks.

Play for the world of Camus.
Let your slender fingers
scatter affection
like lime
to make a visceral pear fertile.

part four

Unto love is art. The congregation
is a hooligan tribe
kneeling before Patron Saints of Selfish Expression
Calliope, Euterpe, and Clio
who are coy with novel and concerto.

Fickle bitches, sisters of promises poorly kept,
they leave the devoted in retail jobs.
Months fall away
while obsessed orphans are lashed
to their chosen form.
Rewrites have too often
shoved other lovers out the door.

It's no mystery why so many
amputate this fancy.

part five

Morpheus: *Good morning.*
I'm off, penniless into the attic.

Awake well, Psyche
as the palette, the choir,
and pretty words pop.
Tulips litter your wrinkled sheet
where this visitor gently trod.

Art is a divine life. It is
to dance. It is to hear God.

tao of miles

the guy is gravity between collaborators on the cover of records
in his image—
not payment's, not the fan's, not the later lines that chased off
previous generations,
his improvs came and went
in gruff instructions towards men with disruptive souls, magic
souls, prodigies emulating the turmoil hendrix shucked off at
woodstock

he's undiscovered chords, a continent full of wraiths rooted too
thoroughly to exorcise, a bully sustaining vibrant life by hitting
piano players
in a boxing ring, like jack johnson throwing hell at a world that
tried to deny him nice cars,
troubled love, miles makes it up both bold and
deep as cathedral pipes
to burn out in the 1970's chugging past subway stations, into
concrete
technicolor, squeamish godfathers would've retired used up,
always reminiscing,

his deeper-than-blue pulled through, the brew reborn heavy
with
complicated scissor fingers,
hip hop,
jazzmen who didn't like to be called "anchors," the ship sliced
choppy water
landing in a stuffy land, a study of men swimming in cocaine,
his tones rose, ballet dancers came, quit work, then left years
after his
compulsion to reinvent, to challenge, fame fading
like distant screams as england's kids with monk-cuts
arrived

another 20 years
the instruments gleamed like an intravenous
legion of half notes, huffing through damaged lips, an ego
that remained rude, in control, drawing off picasso, getting an
electric guitar off 49th street
as nations met, dripped in layers,
a man's best in bourbon distributed at the smooth end of
tumblers
for quintets, quartets, to french women, to the drunk cop in
new york,
seeing music from noise, dwelling on past wives, what's next,
roll the tape

Bebop

Bird and Dizzy
bound out of the doghouse
like fuming dialogue between enemies.
Flaring from a short-lived brotherhood,
captains of beatnik, Bird didn't fly.

Outcasts, cotton became concerts
where white people sat in the back
looking over Nubian heads.
Genuine men made hurricanes sing.

Latin America, Cuban licks succeeded in
thickening a viscous music that keeps
euphony thrust upward, never lonely,
accepted on its own in blown cheeks
and bent brass.

coltrane's flight of myth

you can't avoid the story of a southern boy, marble edges over
blood,
                         the abrasive sound, the wife he left too soon,
            the rat-tat-boom that was antagonism to create fresh religions
                he played in those rooms, in studios, stages, bigger crowds
        saw his unquenchable sax, claiming us all, those righteous hands
a fury
still collecting alms for the sober prodigal son

                coltrane fine-tuned the edge, the out-there cacophony of
                                                                confusion
                    bled out leaving crowds hooked on the coattails of
            races with free jazz, with mortality, taking a precious cluster of
                                                            great blokes
            up as the rising sun with those mad sheets of music, up, up, up,
                    we adore those years of impulse, shaved mouth pieces,
        a life not to be picked apart, not dissected like a list of pleasures
                                                            and grudges
            and nights in cities whose dive bars made a womb of a room
        safe from idiot fans, record executives, young musicians who
                                                        wouldn't make it
            vishnu, shiva, buddha came on tour in the 1950s, after
                                carnegie hall,
                running out of time because of street-bought hustlers,
        humility in such a hoppin' child billowed with age,
        borrowed from constructs just as rebellious a hundred
        years
        earlier
                                                in a viennese world
            that wore white wigs, showed up late, demanded worship,
            but not this one, such was a byproduct, not the point,
            not him, no, the cool, cool karmic transformation of a
            driven man

out of the second chair, obsessive, out of slavery, out
of a
student's life,

        it's now seen as a pilgrimage, as *supreme*

hard scat, man

this is a scat about grimy pavement between buildings, bums,
hunger, half-demolished,
wrecked by rebellion without drugs, without booze,
without sponsors or lawmen or loathing for drones,
firing off from irreverent mouths, chipped teeth
with rusted hoop-in-nose,
screaming, ripped-out-of-the-frame, middle finger up indignant,

slamming on a september evening, england, sex without pistols,
a nowhere kind of handshake, eating huevos rancheros, this
state,
this room
swelling with dodgy irish blokes,
green hair off amps third- or fourth-generation
pawn-shop-
owned,
fist in the air, angry circle storming forward,
the riot that can't be put off when jobs ask too much,
politics too much,
never quiet, thinking how shitty it is to whine in momma's
house,
those old guitarists slip away unnoticed, in need of

one good warehouse fire to be a legend,
a night ranting with the men, it's the revenge for disco,
piss off, shiver, you sheep, you still have my steel switchblade,
jack-o,
i admit it's long done, hateful, peaceful, smiling through and
through
to old girlfriends sleeping with
calmed-down house cats, children, *screw this*, more fists
to the microphone, *more, more, more*
until it's too loud and too late to live

jumping like violent criminals
on the floor below a low ceiling, shaved heads, vultures, mice,
lemurs,
goddamned posers that can't hear, won't look, need
bad knuckles to their soft throats,
all that and this is where black fingernails end
up,
i have no fans to rage
on

the cotton club and shootin' for you

his need to run from a dixie hole put him in a barely better
home,
a city that allowed quasi-happiness, cheering,
shows moving from london to chicago while technique and
velocity became nuance

                    armstrong smoked weed with coffee,
          catapulted by the mob to open doors, revenues, and fame
                              so movies would reel out
                       by his trumpet and earthy baritone

one evening his blessed madam calming came out of a club
and into a waiting cab,
'pops', bumbling over himself and bass players, made a
ballroom for love,
his heart swollen and hers, joyous confetti, she, that louisiana
princess,
the last wife left a detail,

                    the jaunt to new york, in germany he sang too,
                              eisenhower wasn't
                         ready to kill jim crow
                as europe never blinked, africa suffered,
                              america ambivalent,
          disgusted, it remained his bare-chested feeling for the
                                                        south,
                         a pale nemesis

he shoveled so much of himself out, gone, given, free-for-the-
most-part,
an anti-tommy hiding as a hip cat
with this broad, intelligent smile, stoic opinions
making governments call out *communist*
while his music won the war

revolutions

part one

the heavy breath of north carolina evangelicals blew a cat,
    pushed him up, out from unknowing, past carnegie
            hall,
   to tune language played from the hands, the whole body
            twisted,
    stomping feet while drummers smiled at producers
             in
sunglasses
monk's performance writhing under the influence drew worried
eyes,
     sideways melodies, incendiary ivory, a quirky
          omnipotence ruled,
   but by the by-and-by an orpheus slipped out early,
salvaged his purity,
busy arms crossed,
     monk tucked his notes
     in a piano,
   left with a hermit's knapsack,
   adored into death by pannonica

part two

only the holy one knew her,
lady day, the siren, delicious anguish in every song,
pieces of her were stuffed behind the ears of lovers hip on jive,
     blood hungry,
   her cabaret card revoked because too much cool was
      addictive,
      all taking,
wrecked, still adored was polyhymnia
coming back, then giving out,

her heart the property of myth, saddening the husk of us,
just sad,
50-dollar bills taped to her thighs

bullets, books, and regret

angry threats, trash cans thrown through bedroom windows,
beatings in traffic,
gods half open doors between raving and loathing,
all of them laughing
bullets crammed in both pockets,
knuckles split, a baseball bat firms
flesh tired of indecision,
of nostalgia
as the years reach 30, 31, 32
under a .38 in the glovebox,
great-aunt's sheet music is held with red thread.
driver's seat the color of whitewashed walls,
a wedding band is on its edge
littering this here and now.

dear maturity, enemy of buffoons,
that reminds me i was once decent
it's mauled open, strangled, mangled, exploited
like little girls abandoned beside a circus tent.
this is not my country. this is not my dream.

it's a bitch's playground begging for a coup
between college degrees and monster truck chumps
where battalions are met with amphetamines, motorcycles,
and a zeal to hate the self-reliant, the sexy librarian,
the poet bartender
voltaire lashes out, leaps up, a manifesto is written,
its fangs a tiger
to chew through brittle excuses for/against war
friends who share these high stakes are respectfully less-than-
gentlemen,
bake under a harvest moon; loyal new hell heroes.
tranquility is an antediluvian tramp,

the addiction, the harlot of authors.
it's bigger than a cadillac, than threats of terrorism,
than burning crosses; more vast than contempt.
this daily grind sees demons, breathes lilac,
its prerequisites are to bark at strangers and chase fast cars
with hearts punched by railroad spikes.

the mercy of it not working out

late night surgery beneath black candles and tiki mask
lunging, puncturing one lung, then another,
absence is love's wasting virus, engorged with oxygen,
saying a month ago my everything was elsewhere

> i decided it was too rough,
> decided i had poured out,
> it's a wicked bond i have
> to this duty,
> my charge

> pressing my forehead to glass
> in winter,
> there's nothing past steam
> to december
> wing me mercury, the world threatens my quiet
> at its peril

> come sit with me, little bit,
> persuade things to grow, a rainbow,
> wearing pajamas with koi on the sleeves,
> you're a miner's light

come euphoria,
come crescent-moon-and-star,
come meek shoulders and roman soldiers
clashing over the cult of christ,
our arms cozy over anarchy
we are holy ground

> for me tomorrow
> is an infinite devotion to bach
> and tangerines
> resounding over the grand canyon, bouncing eastward,

lonely troubadour,
stand up,
brush off your palms and knees,
around loins to calves empty without
strong hands

the detachment

turn down knobs on the beast, on the indecipherable code,
on ballads
that cause a scuffle, it's an inability to hold still, to take the mind
off this,
this,
this open-ended language of detachment,
unbathed big words
cheap as bazooka bubble gum whose taste is shorter lived,
a slow translation which can't contain it all, its nucleus
is on a
slope,
a malaise that won't allow anyone to improve,
to beat the last generation,
to gain control, to wear one mask,
a desire grows to quit tact, chivalry, pleasantries,
to be that flavor of strange
no one likes

. . .

with belt marks from old beatings, running towards hot trouble,
listening to elvis,
playing texas hold 'em, screaming about the ridiculous end,
sinners lay back among apple trees
and read heaven through fruit-heavy branches,
up there there's an excuse for everything; no need for an alibi

thunder undulates over two lovers,
a man transcends, curves in worship,
she stretches out in a little death under warm rain,

the hood of their car
is an altar

lightning shows their shadows
delighting in this storm, winding down, drenched,
they grow spent,
smoking home with the windows up,
babes of exodus

Sunlight Carves My Chaos

I drag a dread behind my walking,
feeling that worsens with dawn's damned knocking.
At the hour lovers slip out, snags caught in their stockings,
morning dew is a sickness, its presence mocking
my splendor in the silver seconds before sunrise,
crushed by early birds, then Christians in neckties.

      The sun stubbornly returns eager to tell
      the regular man to rise, and me to be still.
      Sun's harsh feet do stomp with ruthless thrill,
      imps scratching daybreak across my windowsill.
      Absent of night I'm befuddled as Hamlet's father,
      pretending the noon-day-mundane isn't a bother.

        Oozing around these thick shades I see,
        that dress socks are in someone else's family tree.
        Come twilight hours! Cupid sings for clubs and G-strings.
        To undulating concrete, a stormy, starry sea,
        searching out Psyche dancing in oblivion,
        me in command of the Flying Dutchman.

Nocturnal morals allow vanity, gluttony, and lust.
I accept the monster, the virgin, and the elasticity of trust.
Under this moonlit grace
floods color, the lark, and her face.
Madam Midnight, the rabble has bedded down.
I don't have to be the charmer, the saint, the clown.

      I am an alchemy of odd hours,
      the innocent devil's helper,
      no conscience, no witnesses,
      a happy social leper.

zen in the time of clockwork hearts

heard over rv parks and deer hunters,
the manic heart carries oboe, kools, and cello
to cobbled-together mountain homes,
                        towards villas nestled in rio de janeiro
                            preserved by scythe and sword,

there are unrequited text messages
rattling like chains, dangling before
being pushed off by piscean intuition

                carry brass knuckles mummified by grime, learn the
                                                        rumba,
                            absent black-out evenings,
                                fool's ink leaves
                        wild ones speaking in terms
                    of ritalin abuse and southern comfort,
                    to speak of it is a sweaty conversation

rise to be self-destructive,
get in line to enter seneca's exit,
to be the new son of a devious family,
a nephilim closing las vegas,

                slip out bedroom windows,
                and scramble to find us an island
                    where there's no more noise

III. The Gateman's Hymn of Ignoracium

Quando noi fummo sor l'ultima chiostra
di Malebolge, sic he I suoi converse
potean patean parere alla venduta nostra,
lamenti saettaron me diversi,
che di pieta ferrati avian li strali;
ond'lo li orecchi con le mani copersi.

—Dante Alighieri, *Divine Comedy, Inferno*

My Confession in Your Dreams

Climb astride cushions.
Curl into an oneiric cocoon.
Sleep as Bosch washes athwart the walls.
Hear this myth begin to breathe.

. . .

Inferno, Purgatory, and Paradise,
where spirits were once made or sacrificed,
have been given another brother.
Humans decided Hell hadn't enough horror
and so earned this charred mirror.
God gave them an unknown end,
a city infinite and numb,
my glorious Ignoracium.

And I, the youngest son of Empyrean,
am The Gateman.

My place here is a negotiated plea:
I become the Eternal Helmsman
of these gnashing machines,
and He forgets I didn't fight.
I stand as the inheritor
of gears which digest guests,
souls Morning Star won't *savoir.*

Whimper on this spot, you dead, you cannibals!

The sun is blind to my tribes,
the moon a stark, frozen pockmark.
Each morning a smoldering scar
shines gray

and folks arrive clutching mythology.
Wind separates their ability to pray,
and whittles hope from their bones.
Tractor tires blaze,
searing skin in a waxen haze.

My lack of love
leaves them gaunt.

Men's infected ids were once hidden
behind art, business, or religion.
Here, exposed, they slither in single-file.
The Creator isn't listening.
Meet the lads and ladies flickered out
wailing, howling, and twitching.

Soldiers of the Gateman

Beware: I've enlisted Medusa's sisters.
Hobgoblins carry blow torches into these fissures.
A chimera of ancient gods,
they have come wearing gore and grins
delighted to be believed again.
Ignoracium is a legion of folklore.

The bloodline of my lupine warriors
is pure.
Cyclops and Manananggal breed more mongrels.
Hate quakes before this crew of regret.
Who better than a dragon
and the Kraken
to raze this place that never forgets?

Platoons of Akvan and Windigo
lashed out above now do so below.
Humanity's faces flail in a gale
throwing blades of sand.
Uncatchable mouths at their ankles,
ice splinters in callous ears.
My wolves are the weather
living drunk on tears.

From a marriage of Mamu and Eloko
is this union in devotion to me.
I raise my own masochistic employees.
Vomit not, this serpentine lot
is no less in God's plan than man,
than you.
I need help
to sustain this grim Eden.

As summer comes,
as winter sobs,

as trees bear arms
the kingdom swings an ax.
Gryphons descend in a herd.
Tribulation is a perpetual blizzard.

They tell tall tales
after tearing each heart apart.
They are Revelation's inspiration
creating a symphony that rivals Mozart.

Pious Hypocrites

They are circus monkeys
reading verses to hide their venom.
Frauds here are brutally forsaken.
At barren tables these spirits are naked
doomed to dine on soot.
They peeled apart Proverbs
to preach a lesson most imbalanced.
On earth they were an infinite hindrance,
harlequins juggling vice with their Bibles.

That financial hobnobbing in church
is cashed in here, reputation besmirched.
Crusaders! Come forward,
you clan of vapid vessels
who took to the pulpit
to spread sexist offal and racist shit.
Self-serving belief is viler
than admitting doubt or even denial.
Those earthly pews have rotted through.

This is Vishnu's nightmare.

Facades are shattered in Ignoracium.
Imps in tuxedos serve irony through stingy tubes.
The elite's garments are snatched off,
their carcasses consumed
into a multitude of tummies disinherited.
The Helpless now help masticate
those indolent thighs and double chins.

Pious Hypocrites: jesters and missionaries
who didn't care, noisy banners blown by hot air.
You held out wooden nickels

for fools and old women seeking leeway.
In life you sat on golden thrones.
Perished, jewels are traded for a gasoline bidet.
Your lukewarm intent was your undoing.
Oh false prophets, what was the cost?

They are poor here. They are hungry.
They are lost.
Obsessively, they inscribe the King James,
the Koran, the Bhagavad Gita
all the scripture misquoted in vanity's name.
They scribble with a scalpel on the back
in front of them, perpetual first drafts.
Furrowed brows burdened in freezing rooms,
the words they compulsively craft
quickly vanish.

None understands the other.
Speaking only glossolalia with no merit,
so many Cassandras now see truth in the Spirit
a lifetime too late.
Their only goal is to rip and rewrite
again and again and again.
Insanity does my copy room maintain.

Malignant Merchants

Green-eyed merchants
blink blindly,
sinking in the Sea of Misappropriations.
Adlet sprint in a desert valley
with fluttering clouds of currency
behind paws of post-life inflation.
Villainous businessmen follow
bedeviled, panting, scratching, sockets hollow.
They are slaves for blank paper.

No rest, onward still at my behest,
even when their strength begins to taper.
Slashed by swords of volcanic glass
intestines beneath their feet do dangle.
The selfish try upon try
to buy their way out
while becoming more entangled.

Here these thieves
are in an office windowless,
repaying their victims with pain.
Those in line are eager to twist and tear
these greedy who lived most inhumane
and wrench out clumps of hair.
Every hand is staked to a desk.
In dire straits they were mute.
No pity only averages, choosing sales,
now here wearing burlap suits.
Their Darwinian theory attacked itself,
the most savage survived,
not the strongest.

Hermes mocks these men as his reproduction.

Their faces stretched out like a drum,
pounded by wicked elves while they hum
landing a maelstrom of steel-forged strikes.
Bankrupt, pin-striped lawyers
cannot cajole enough to save themselves.
This end, for this Ode to Sin,
there are no appeals.

As the cruelest show,
a keyhole is torn in the ceiling
so they see
how family sold their tainted fortune.
An accumulation cast off
for a paltry fee.
Their children
leave the father's memory
only on a headstone.
Vipers don't honor their departed.

Monsters

For monsters, soulless butchers,
I provide the hardest bed.
I staple open greasy eyelids
while swollen organs are tied off with threads.
All of Heaven's fondled,
demeaned Little Ms. Beauty Queens
show up for retribution.
Delicate fairies, stolen, buried in thickets,
now howl down to collect restitution.

Children thrash on rapists like rabid bats.
A murder of metallic crows, justified hellcats,
lightning bolts and chainsaws,
attrition is a dish served severed.
Molesters are my creatures' favorite flavor.

Caligula, under my insignia
you are resurrected here.
Lead these baboons obsessed with pigtails
into a flurry of teeth and cat o' nine tails.
Gnaw through their throats,
and exit out that fetid instrument.
Torn, torn again, aware of each detail,
press on! Let the beasts meet themselves.

Cold bedrooms where blue eyes
were abused
here see their predator prostrate.
Impaled by Nimrod freed from gibbering slavery,
his phallus, the rest of their fate,
is slid down Vlad's pike.
Scores of skulking midnight-men skewered.

Edwards' spider thread does strangle you.

Wail for those tragic, septic ways,
starved hyenas, playground wraiths.
These trolls are swung from their toes
and drowned at sunset.
Remorseless, sneaking, incestuous cancers,
nightfall is an eel, my awful vignette.
Tails are pincers, a razor to the sphincter,
stinging into exsanguination.

It is never different. It is not
for liberal leanings.
Morons wish the heels would stop stomping,
but without them I'd have no meaning.
Satyrs keep them busy.
From toenails to temple
they are peeled.
Malformed souls, purged from earth,
at my altar they now kneel.

I torment the innocent-eaters.
I take from those who took from precious youth.
Even Hades halts its business
to sneer at these sniveling uncouth.
These, my sorry inventory,
with Gacy's Pa Pa Midnight flung in here—
their ceaseless rape is my opiate-shot glory.

Rest at Ease, Good Heart

I am agony, inebriated now
that we share this truth, my admission,
my Ignoracium.

I am an independent.
Not a Fallen, no second rate indigent,
I am forged from swords
wielded in that Great Battle,
wearing crowns of thorns
around my wrists.
Whether by war or cross,
thirty coins or ill-fated tryst,
any of the Seven,
the special ones come to me.
I am the bastard son of Heaven.

I do not adore you.
Toast not in my blood,
parched, marooned ones.

I am the Reaper's grandfather.
Seraphs refuse to walk where I've trod.
I am fused from scars, licked by wounds,
the brainchild of Marquis de Sade.
I am Ignoracium's Almighty.
Goodnight. Sleep well.
Keep my secret, never tell.
Trust the morbidly gorgeous god of maggots,
who's patient in the space evil's mercy inhabits.
All your sins are remembered.

Clifford Brooks was born in Athens, Georgia. His first poetry collection, *The Draw of Broken Eyes & Whirling Metaphysics,* was nominated for a Georgia Author of the Year Award in Poetry. His limited-edition poetry chapbook *Exiles of Eden* was published in 2017. Clifford is the founder of The Southern Collective Experience, a cooperative of writers, musicians and visual artists, which publishes the journal *The Blue Mountain Review* and hosts the radio show *Dante's Old South.* He currently lives in northwest Georgia.

www.cliffbrooks.com